WHEN D IS FOR DEPLOYED

BY ELEANOR D. ALSPAUGH

This book is dedicated to my granddaughter Savannah, whose love crossed the miles separating her from her Daddy. It is also dedicated to her parents, Ethan and Julianne, and so many other military families. Many thanks to the soldiers who selflessly sacrifice time spent with their own families for the good of our nation; as well as to the many back home that tirelessly keep the family fires and love burning. Like my own parents during World War II, their love transcends the distance apart.

My name is Savannah
and my Daddy is a soldier.
This picture was taken when I was just a baby.

I was little when we learned Daddy would be deployed.
Being deployed meant that he would be on military
duty helping to keep our country safe. He would
be stationed far away in another country.

I wondered why and how long Daddy would be gone.
Daddy would not be able to come home after work or
on weekends. I wondered what I would do while Daddy
was deployed. Before he left, I stored up on snuggles and fun.
When Daddy held me close, I thought he would
never let me go!

As a soldier, he received orders to serve our country. After Daddy left, Mama hugged me and that was when our adventure began—Waiting for Daddy to return! It definitely would not be in time for dinner!

Our family and friends rallied around us as we waited
for Daddy to come home.

You have to hang on tightly with my uncle!
I think Daddy would like this kind of play!

My secret comforts are my binky and blankie. Anytime
I snuggle with them, I can pretend my Daddy is holding
me again. But when I'm really tired, a warm Auntie or
Pappy's snuggles help a lot too!

In October, Mama raked leaves. Guess who got to jump in them?
Me! Mama, lots of leaves, binky and me! I was surprised that even
though Daddy was away, I liked Fall! Daddy liked the photos we
shared. He wanted us to have fun while he was deployed.

I wanted Daddy to have fun too! When he called, I took
him into the pile of leaves with me! Leaves were flying
and we were laughing! Then suddenly my phone with
Daddy tumbled! I quickly picked him up and brushed
away the leaves. He smiled and said he was fine. I guess
I will have to hold him tighter next time!

But wait—Fall fun was not over yet!
We went trick-or-treating and to a
parade to celebrate!

There were lots of costumes, parade floats and CaNdY!

We hoped Daddy would not miss us too much at
Thanksgiving -- or the yummy food! Mama made a
care package filled with lots of goodies and love!
I helped decorate the box! We mailed it early so he
would know that near or far, he is always in our thoughts.

Thanksgiving Day was special for another reason too! It was Mama's birthday! Daddy remembered! He sent her a present.

Make a wish Mama that Daddy comes home soon!

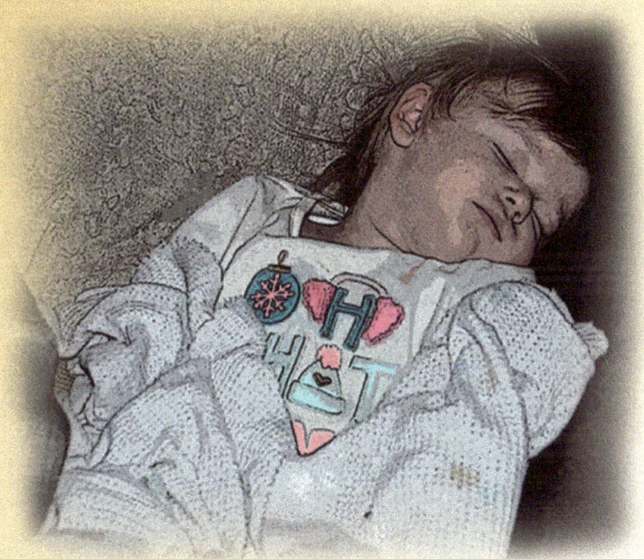

At the end of that busy day, I learned that I can sleep without my Daddy, my binky or even my bed if I'm tired enough!

Most nights before I fell asleep, we prayed that Daddy would come home safely. In the morning, I could be pretty silly playing hide and seek in my bed.

Can you find Savannah???

Here I am!

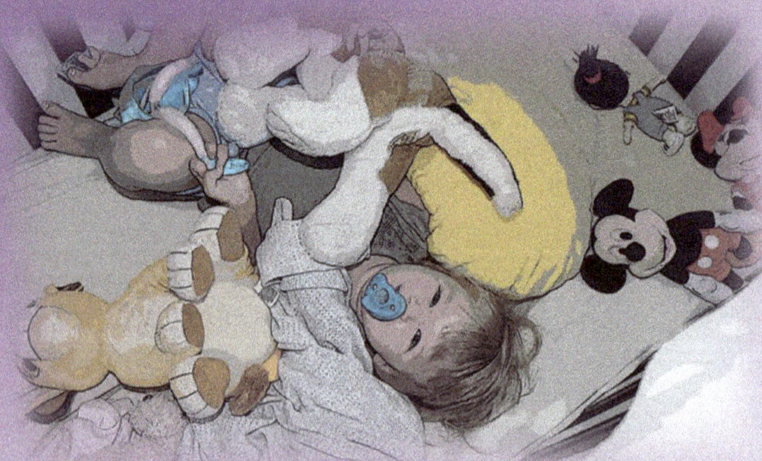

Even though Daddy was far away, he was thinking of me.
He sent a video of him reading this book to me.
I loved hearing him read to me again!
He also sent a pillowcase with his picture on it.
We found a place of honor for it!

We hung it in my room
right above my bed where
Daddy could watch over me.

In December, I held a holiday tea party for the pups!
They love having tea especially if treats are being served!

Welcome Puppies!

I'm glad you could come! One treat or two?
Be careful not to spill your tea Sammy!

At Christmas time, I also entertained my other Grandparents!
We make each other laugh! Daddy was right there with us
too—Like magic, he could be home with us again!

We rang in the New Year at an ice festival.
HaPpY NEW YEAR!
It's the year Daddy comes HOME!

Every February, I'm always Daddy's
funny Valentine! Near or far,
we love each other very much!

In March, I was playing with my castle when Daddy called!
On Mama's phone, Daddy looked so small, he could fit in
my castle.   He can't do that when he's home!

Even though Mama said it was a long-distance call, we felt close. We had lots of fun together just like we always do!

Sit down Daddy! Welcome Home!
It felt like he was really here with me.

In fact, I thought it would be fun for us to have a snack together.

Open wide Daddy!
Isn't it Yummy?

Now let's share!
My Turn!

In April, we went to the BIGGEST Easter egg hunt
held by my Great Aunt and Uncle. I collected lots of eggs
with my wingman, Daddy right there by my side!

In May, Mama and I attended my Aunt's Graduation.
Then Mama traveled to another country to meet Daddy!
When she came home, she brought me hugs from Daddy.

In June, my cousin Lucy was born! Spending time with
sweet baby Lucy helped the days pass quickly!

In July, we got a special surprise! On Daddy's birthday,
he started the long trip home to us! Mama and I
made welcome home signs. Mama bought a special
dress for me to wear when we would finally welcome
Daddy home.

When Daddy returned, he was much bigger than he looked in that little phone!

Daddy reached out his hand
to gently touch me and reassure me
that he was really home, safe and sound.

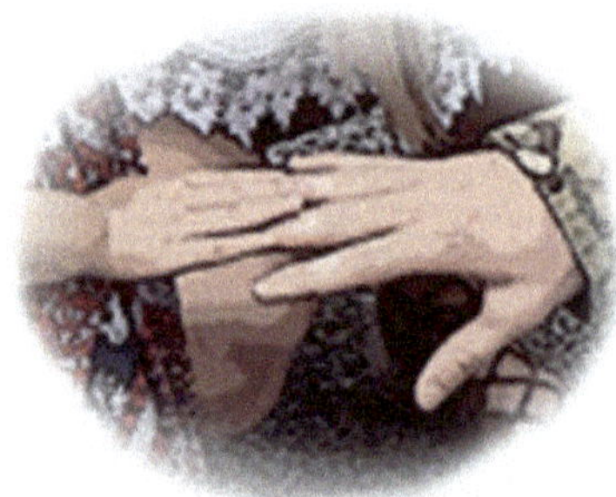

As Daddy headed for the house, I caught a ride
on his duffel bag!

Before long, we were playing
and hugging and so very
happy!

My Daddy was
home,
safe and sound!

Get ready!! Here I come Daddy!!
We Missed You Ethan!

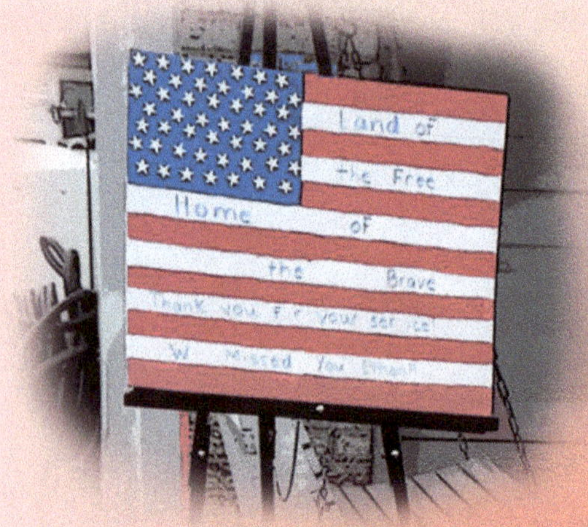

Daddy missed us while he was away but he is proud to be a soldier and serve our country. If Daddy is deployed again, I know that no matter how far apart we are, we will find ways to be together.

Welcome Home Daddy!
We are so proud of you and love having you home!

Eleanor Donald Alspaugh was raised in Hatboro, Pennsylvania and graduated from Shippensburg University. Formerly an Assistant Vice President, she became a multi-award-winning author after she captured the antics of raising her three children while surviving life as a wife and working mother in *The Mommy-Go-Round*, a humorous and heartwarming account of motherhood, childhood and everything in between. She has been a long-time resident of Carlisle, Pennsylvania, where she resides with her husband Stephen and family. In addition to the release of *When D is For Deployed* in 2022, Eleanor has worked extensively on a second book entitled *The Heart of a Soldier* which is scheduled for release in early 2022. In this book, Eleanor shares her decorated father's letters home during World War II, as well as her parents' love story set against historic highlights and issues of World War II. Eleanor is currently a part-time photographer, author, caregiver, not to mention Mother and Grandmother. With completion of the two most recent books, Eleanor looks forward to spending more time completing a sequel to *The Mommy-Go-Round* as well as a second children's book.